PLANNING SUGGESTIONS

1. Ask God to bless and guide you as you consider what's most helpful to bring families in your community closer to him in the coming months.
2. Glance through the four sessions so that you have an overview of the months ahead, noting down resources that will take time to source.
3. Use the downloadable planning sheets to share this month's session with your core team in plenty of time, and meet to shape the ideas together to suit your own situation.
4. If you're meeting face to face with the team, talk about this month's theme, using the Messy team theme provided.
5. Tell God your worries.
6. Ensure that the whole extended team has copies of your final version of activities, together with the Bible reflection provided to give them the background they need. You could give them the link to the passage on www.biblegateway.com if you're not certain they have their own Bibles.
7. Include the take-home ideas on handouts, texts or a Facebook page to join.
8. Print copies of the mealtime question cards for the meal tables.
9. Encourage review and reflection from everyone after the session has taken place and respond to suggestions for change ready for next time.
10. Thank God for wherever you saw him at work.

Send in news, stories and photos to messychurch@brf.org.uk

To order back issues of *Get Messy!* and Messy Church resources, email BRF on **enquiries@brf.org.uk** or telephone **01865 319700**

For general enquiries contact our Messy Church administrator on 01235 858246 or email **messychurch@brf. org.uk**

THEMES IN THIS E

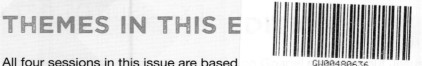

All four sessions in this issue are based ... range from focusing on Jesus at just a f... and resurrection.

In **January** we look at the delightful cross-generational story of Mary and Joseph taking Jesus to the Temple. The baby, the teenage mum, the older dad and the comparatively ancient Anna and Simeon meet in the arms of the Holy Spirit.

In **February** we step into the Last Supper, which you might see as a prompt to explore how to share Holy Communion in your Messy Church, or simply as a key story that helps us understand Jesus' cross and resurrection.

Easter is in **March** this year and our Good Friday/Easter Day Messy Church invites a pause for wonder at the empty tomb. Not bunnies. Avoid bunnies. You might want to check out *Messy Easter* for additional ideas (see overleaf).

And in **April** we step back into Jesus' time in Jerusalem before the crucifixion, when we enjoy the story of the widow giving her tiny-but-huge offering. It is an opportunity to explore the themes of justice and kingdom values as well as to see Jesus at his most compassionate and respectful towards the most vulnerable in society.

CONTENTS

IN THE NEXT ISSUE OF *GET MESSY*!

MAY: OUR WORLDWIDE FAMILY

JUNE: THE VALLEY OF DRY BONES

JULY: HANDLING OUR WORRIES

AUGUST: TEAM JESUS

NEW FROM BRF

CORE SKILLS FOR FAMILY MINISTRY

978 085746 431 6
£12.99

User-friendly modular training course for children's and family work practitioners—with a session written by Messy Church's very own Martyn Payne!

Core Skills for Family Ministry is an interdenominational modular scheme offering foundational training for all those involved with church-based family ministry.

It offers six stand-alone sessions on:

- Biblical, historical and contemporary understanding of family
- Family ministry today
- Seasons of family life
- Role of family relationships
- Family wellbeing and wholeness
- Faith in families

All six modules have been field-tested as pilot sessions with participants from different denominations. Each module is creative, thought-provoking, interactive and designed to inspire and refresh children's and family workers at all levels of expertise and experience.

To order or find out about other resources, visit **www.brfonline. org.uk**

AND DON'T FORGET

MESSY EASTER

978 1 84101 717 4
£6.99

CREATIVE IDEAS FOR LENT AND EASTER

978 0 85746 245 9
£8.99

A NOTE ABOUT THE SESSION MATERIAL

After careful consultation, we've decided not to continue with the handout sheets and to incorporate 'Sunday treat' into 'take-home ideas'. We hope you approve! If you have any ideas for improvements to this magazine, do email us at messychurch@brf.org.uk.

WHY NOT VISIT

WWW.INF.CO.UK/ INFINITE/MESSY-CHURCH-EASTER.HTML

FOR EASTER CRAFT IDEAS?

Get Messy!

JAN–APR 2016

SESSION MATERIAL, NEWS, STORIES AND INSPIRATION FOR MESSY CHURCHES

THE MESSY CHURCH MAGAZINE

SESSIONS IN THIS ISSUE:

Past, present and future
The last supper
Unbelievable truth
Two tiny coins

MESSY MONASTICS? • THE GREAT BIG BRF MESS-ABOUT! • JOINING GENERATIONS

Messy Church® is a registered word mark and the logo is a registered device mark of The Bible Reading Fellowship

Get Messy! © BRF 2016
ISBN 978 0 85746 404 0
All rights reserved

The Bible Reading Fellowship
15 The Chambers, Vineyard,
Abingdon OX14 3FE

Tel: +44 (0)1865 319700
Fax: +44 (0)1865 319701

Email: enquiries@brf.org.uk
Website: www.brf.org.uk

BRF is a Registered Charity

Acknowledgements

Scripture quotations marked (GNT) are taken from the Good News Translation copyright © 1992 by American Bible Society.

Scripture quotations marked (NCV) are taken from The Holy Bible, New Century Version®. Copyright © 2005 by Thomas Nelson, Inc.

Unless otherwise stated, scripture quotations are taken from The Holy Bible, New International Version (Anglicised edition), copyright © 1979, 1984, 2011 by Biblica (formerly International Bible Society), and are used by permission of Hodder & Stoughton Publishers, an Hachette UK company. All rights reserved. 'NIV' is a registered trademark of Biblica (formerly International Bible Society). UK trademark number 1448790.]

Editor: Olivia Warburton

Subeditor: Jenni Dutton

Designer: Rebecca J Hall

Proofreader: Michelle Clark

Cover photos: Renita Boyle

Printed in the UK by Stephens & George Print Group

Note for subscribers

Print copies are dispatched to arrive six weeks prior to the date on the cover of the magazine. The May 2016 issue should be with you around the middle of March 2016. The PDF version of the magazine is also available for purchase and immediate download from the beginning of March 2016.
www.messychurch.org.uk/ resources/get-messy

Photocopying

You're welcome to photocopy the Bible reflections and session outlines for use only within your team. Copying other parts of the magazine is not permitted.

MEET OUR SESSION AND BIBLE STUDY WRITERS FOR THIS ISSUE

Sian Ashford is part of the kids' leadership team at Ivy Church in Manchester. Her Messy Church adventure started two years ago, and she and the team have loved welcoming families from all walks of life through the doors. With a husband, three children and a dog at home, it is rare that the mess stays at church!

Pete Maidment is the Diocesan Youth Adviser for the Diocese of Winchester, and heads up Messy Church training in the diocese. He is part of the core leadership team for the Messy Church that meets at St Wilfrid's Church in Cowplain, where he devises some of the more wacky crafts! Pete is married and has two children who are crazy about Messy Church. In his spare time Pete is a keen runner and drinks more coffee than is probably good for him.

Becky May lives in Bedfordshire with her husband and her young son, Isaac. She is a Messy Church Regional Coordinator and is involved in running the Messy Church at Wixams Church, Bedford, having previously led and supported a range of different children's and youth activities. She feels very much at home with anything messy!

Debbie Peatman belongs to a Messy congregation in Morecambe, and is Regional Coordinator for Messy Churches in Lancashire. When not busy baking in the local pie shop, she is working on her first novel. She is married to Mike, has two children and lives in a very messy rectory.

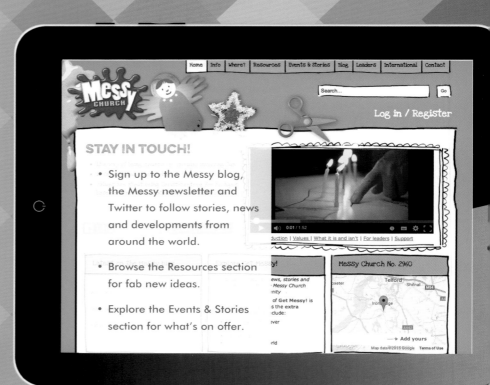

 **MessyChurchBRF**    **MessyChurchBRF**   **@MessyChurchBRF**

JOINING GENERATIONS

LET'S ASK INSTEAD, 'HOW MANY PEOPLE CAME TODAY?'

I have a lovely photo from our Messy Church. A teenage boy stands staring thoughtfully, his hands ready for action, by a table at which a dad, his child and another child are working together with intense concentration on something gooey. Meanwhile a silver-haired woman, bursting with energy, leans over to give them a helping hand. In the background, there are similar groupings, similarly occupied. Nothing dramatic is happening; it's just an everyday scene, and I expect you have many comparable photos from your Messy Church. But what I love about it is the way it reveals how our church sees God and his kingdom.

The photo is reminiscent of Andrei Rublev's *Icon of the Trinity*, in which three angelic figures sit round a table, utterly engrossed in each other and in what they're doing. Although the group is complete and its members satisfied by themselves, they are still open to being joined by outsiders, as the empty side of the table shows. Both this and the photo are pictures of missional community, of an enjoyable experience enhanced by the presence of others who are similar yet different. They are pictures of equality without conformity, of gracious sharing, living and learning together. Here there is space for new relationships to be risked and old ones rewoven—and both pictures involve food! In the photo, I love the way the proximity of four generations seems to shout of eternity: faithfulness in the past, joy in the present and hope for the future. That's why the all-age aspect of Messy Church is so important and will continue to be so. It's often misunderstood, sold short and taken for granted. So let's celebrate it again here!

Non-verbal communication—the actions, attitudes and environment that demonstrate clearly what we really believe—goes on in any form of church. We can talk all we like about how much Jesus valued children and how he invited a child to stand in the disciples' midst as an example of discipleship, but then if we design our services around the preferences of adults only, and send children out of our main church gathering, what message is *actually* being communicated? If we design a church for children alone, there is a danger that all of us, including the children, understand the message to be 'Christianity is only for children. You'll grow out of it. Christianity is only relevant until you're eleven. It has nothing to say to adults.' This is not only unhelpful for today's adults, who then have every excuse to sit in the back row during the celebration and catch up with emails while the children 'have their little sing-song', but it also sows seeds in the children of expecting to give it all up when they grow up. If, instead, adults and children experience a community in which children, teens, adults and the elderly are all engaged, excited, committed and valued, an unspoken expectation is set that you will be an important and useful member of this community for your whole life.

'We had 34 children today.' We see this on so many Facebook reports, and it implies a deep-seated belief that actually we're only doing Messy Church for the children and adults don't count, literally. The logical end result of this attitude is that the activities, celebration and meal will all be orientated more and more towards the children alone, and the adults will merely become undervalued babysitters. Let's ask instead, 'How many PEOPLE came today?'

So, at your next Messy Church, take a moment to notice the mystery of those apparently ordinary intergenerational moments round the tables. Take a moment to thank God for bringing young and old together against all the odds. Glory for a moment in the way his kingdom is one where we are valued from the moment of our conception to beyond our final breath. Treasure the demonstration all around you that in Christ's family you are loved and needed, whatever you look like, whatever your abilities and disabilities, whether you're at the start of life's journey or near the end. The Church proves you are eternally loved.

Katrina Thomas, Children in URBan Situations (CURBS)

In a church hall in Leicester, it is Monday afternoon and the place is silent. Tables are out, crafts are prepared and there is a loaf of bread for making toast on the counter. Then the door down the corridor opens and a dad, mum and daughter walk in, talking about their day. They sign in and, as I look up and smile, the dad says, 'Have you burned down any schools this week?' Everyone laughs and I say, no, not this week, before offering them a hot drink while their daughter runs to see what activities we have planned today. This is how every Craft Café has started since a dad and I nearly burned down the church kitchen, and it will probably continue to do so until something more exciting takes over the memories of those who attend.

Craft Café is a ministry of St Christopher's Church in Leicester and takes place every Monday in term time. The church, uniquely, occupies part of the building of a Church of England academy for children from three to 16 years old, which draws pupils from two estate communities. Craft Café was started in 2008 to provide families with somewhere to go after school to do crafts, to hear more about God and to share food. It is Messy Church, but has a few subtle differences, which I see when travelling around and speaking to various churches as part of my role with CURBS as Project Coordinator.

CURBS is a Christian organisation that has been resourcing urban children's work for 20 years, providing support, resources and training. CURBS came from a desire to produce resources that were different from mainstream ones—to look from the perspective of children's spirituality while being aware of their particular urban living environment in deprived areas, acknowledging both struggles and successes. There are CURBS hubs in cities all over the country, where those working with children and families are able to meet to share best practice and ideas. Many of these people are running expressions of Messy Church.

Messy Church has been a huge blessing to those working in deprived contexts because it meets a need that is often missed by statutory services—the need for a space in which all ages are welcomed and supported; a space for the community it is in. In this sense the CURBS approach and Messy Church walk hand in hand, so it is no great surprise that churches using CURBS resources often do so in a 'Messy style'.

So how is urban Messy Church distinct from the usual Messy Church model? There are three elements in which differences can be seen in many urban contexts: **frequency**, **food** and **formality**.

FREQUENCY

A number of urban Messy Church expressions occur much more regularly than the once-a-month model because of community needs. I know that if St Christopher's Craft Café was monthly the families attending would a) have nothing else to do in that time slot on a weekly basis and b) forget to come. The weekly pattern means it is part of a family's rhythm, so, although the group is small, attendance is regular. The celebration and crafts are linked to the previous Sunday's church theme, so both the Sunday and Messy Church congregations are hearing the same message, but often in very different ways.

FOOD

Food is a challenge when meeting more than once a month, both in terms of the volunteers involved with making and serving it and in terms of the cost. In many areas it is difficult to ask families to contribute to the cost of a meal because they simply do not have money to spare and so wouldn't come along. So, in order to have a meal as part of their session, many urban Messy Churches are being a bit creative, and the humble toaster, jam and white sliced loaf have been lifted in status to mealtime centrepiece. In some contexts the meal is the most difficult part of the session, as explained by Emma O'Hagan, Youth and Families Missioner and CURBS Champion in the Liverpool Diocese: 'The mealtime is hard for most of

Leicester

MESSY BY A DIFFERENT NAME...

the families that we have come along because they struggle with sitting here around a table, because it just isn't how they eat at home. In order for the families to feel comfortable and keep coming we have to be practical, and so it means that our mealtimes are perhaps more fluid and "messy" than those that other Messy Churches have.'

FORMALITY

I am currently involved with two Messy Churches two miles apart and the difference in structure is startling. One, in a middle-class village, is a very structured monthly session with a vast volunteer team and a sit-down hot meal with a cake-based dessert. The other is a casual café-style setting, with a small volunteer team and a 'toast banquet'. Both Messy Churches may do similar crafts and be looking at the same story, but have very different styles to meet the needs of their communities. Linked to this, a number of urban Messy Churches have chosen not to use the name 'Messy Church', instead using something the community is more able to engage with. For example, in areas where going into a Christian place of worship is difficult from a religious or cultural perspective, choosing a different name can make a Messy Church more acceptable and accessible for the community it serves.

This is the core of the issue: Messy Churches are diverse, and look different in different places to meet the needs of their communities—from those who love nothing better than a meal of sausage and mash to those who avoid it in predominantly Jewish or Muslim areas; from those who love their celebration to be led by a five-piece worship band to those preferring a lone, unamplified guitar. These expressions of Messy Church are just as 'messy' as those appearing to conform to the original model, with messy play and crafts, messy worship, messy food and, most of all, messy lives.

Stories from Messy Churches far and wide

Land's End benefice

Revd Canon Vanda Perrett

Land's End in Cornwall is more than its famous signpost and more than a popular holiday destination. The winter population of our three parishes (St Sennen, St Buryan and St Levan) is around 3000; in the summer this rises to 29,500. We have extremes of poverty and wealth: our schoolchildren are among the poorest in the country, yet we have vast numbers of second-home owners. The poverty of many families in this benefice was a driving factor to set up a Messy Church. There is little for children to do here in the winter months and for families on limited incomes the attractions are a very occasional treat. There is also a great tradition of artists and craftspeople, who often work in isolation.

Our Messy Church began small, as a benefice event. The parishes each contributed money and volunteers, as well as organising their own DBS checks and venues. It is important Messy Church is sustainable, so it is bimonthly, the venue rotating between parishes. We held our first Messy Church in May 2015 and had a range of activities. We worried about the meal; the kitchen was not able to cope with hot meals, so we opted for a picnic tea where everyone made their own sandwiches, decorated cakes and shared them together just before our worship. This worked extremely well. (Gluten-free options were available.) Some primary-aged children had never made sandwiches or decorated fairy cakes before!

I was hoping for 20 people in total, but we actually had 30 people attend. People were really appreciative and some became advocates for our next Messy Church.

What did we learn? Publicity is key—we used Facebook, posters and direct invitations as well as church pew sheets. Now we send flyers home via all local schools—plus we list the next Messy Church on each of the three church websites. We also learned planning and preparation are hard work but essential; a warm smile and a proper welcome go a long way; booking people in takes more time than you think; and to try not to look too surprised when faced with great success—God is blessing this work!

Messy Marquee at the Relay for Life

Renita Boyle describes *Put your Prayers in the Air*

www.relay.cancerresearchuk.org/site/PageNavigator/Home

Cancer affects everyone in every community.

That's why the biannual Dumfries and Galloway Relay for Life held in Wigtown, Scotland raised over £62,000 for Cancer Research UK in 2015 alone.

Relay provides more than vital funds, however. It brings everyone in the community together to show their support and solidarity, celebrate cancer survivors and remember those lost.

Messy Church (Wigtown and Around) set up a Messy Marquee to provide participants with space to breathe, reflect, create and or chat about loved ones lost to or fighting cancer. Throughout the day we made praising arms and hands and added them to our frame for prayer.

'Put your Prayers in the Air' became our slogan as we walked laps with other relayers.

It is hard to describe just how meaningful this was for people; how incarnational it became.

Thank you. It was so peaceful. There was such a presence.

Made us feel that we are not alone.

I liked talking with you about my Granny. I miss her.

Gave us something quiet to do as a family.

It was fun and free!

What a cool tent!

Such support. Thank you for walking laps with us.

You can just feel the hope here.

I would heartily recommend any Messy Church to get involved with their local Relay for Life.

I was so moved and inspired by *Prayers in the Air* and the opportunity it offered Relay participants to celebrate, remember and give hope for their loved ones touched by cancer. It was a wonderful way to enable people to reflect on why they were taking part in Relay in a safe and supportive environment. Thank you so much for taking the time out to be part of the Relay Family and bring the fellowship of the church to us.
Anne Barclay, Committee Chair, Dumfries and Galloway Relay for Life, Cancer Research UK

Messy prayer time

Eileen Ray shares from Australia

We always have a deliberate prayer time at our Messy Church. Usually I hand out battery-operated candles and ask each person to think about what they want to pray for. Then, when they are ready, they place their candle on a special table. Recently one boy had told his mother he didn't want to come, then changed his mind so that the family arrived late—but when I started to hand out the candles he immediately exclaimed, 'Oooh, I love this!' His mother said he had been saying he didn't believe in God, but she asked him to tell her about the God he didn't believe in… I have been taken aback at just how reverently and seriously the children in particular treat prayer time at Messy Church. That one thing makes it worthwhile to me.

LETTER TO THE PHILIPPIANS— REWRITTEN!

WITH APOLOGIES, AND CREDIT FOR ANY GOOD THEOLOGY, TO THE APOSTLE PAUL

Dear Messy Church leaders and Regional Coordinators

Lucy here, writing on behalf of the whole Messy Church team at BRF. Hello! What a great partnership we have in this Messy work God's given us. It's so good to be in this together and, right at the start of this letter, we want to pray God's grace and peace on your work, knowing that you pray the same for us.

We do thank God for you! Every time we think of you, on our own or together at team meetings, we thank him, feeling a bit blown away by the way you give so much to and through your Messy Church. It's tempting to feel overwhelmed by the size of the Messy network and the speed at which it's growing, and to feel frustrated by the fact we can't know every leader personally. It feels as if we can't do our job properly. But we're confident that if it's God who started something in your church, rather than us or even you, he won't stop till he's finished the job to his satisfaction.

(By the way, is it OK to feel a personal involvement with you? Surely it is! Even if we're a long way from each other, even if your Messy Church is only a name on a database or website or a page on Facebook, you're still in our hearts; but I still wish we could all get together and share what God's doing face to face!)

And this is our prayer: we pray you won't compromise on knowledge, understanding or opportunities for learning—for your team as well as for the families who come. We pray you will all have a depth of insight to see what is really real, not what society presents as real. We pray that you will have God's spectacles to see what's best for family and community and church and kingdom in the place where *you* live. And we pray that you will live an exemplary life, that you'll be

people of integrity living out the Gospel and enjoying the good life God has prepared for you, and that Jesus Christ will shine through everything you do.

If people object to Messy Church or think there's a better way to preach Jesus, like putting energies into traditional church, that's OK; we can rejoice in Messy and other sorts of church, because what matters is that Jesus is lived out in the world. We're all in this together—BRF, Messy Church leaders on the ground, the denominations we belong to and the Holy Spirit. BRF is committed to this work of God in his Church: we are committed heart and soul and we want to keep on helping you. You don't actually need us to visit, even if that's encouraging both for you and for us. Just live out the Gospel through your Messy Church. What or who are you frightened of or bugged by? There's no need to be! Opposition is OK—it's kind of trivial in the bigger picture. You can expect God's Messy call on you to be costly, hard work and exhausting, to take its toll on you physically, mentally and emotionally; we can expect to go through difficult patches and to struggle—this is our privilege and our prize. It's God's way of saying we're doing a good job.

Work together on your team. (We do!) Don't expect this team stuff to happen easily. If Jesus means anything to you, then what should be your priority? To love each other, to stick together when you disagree, to remind each other what you're in it for, who you're in it for. Yes, use your own gifts and have fun in this mission, but make sure everyone on the team is having as much fun as you by being the person they were made to be and using their gifts, too. If you can't work out how, go back to Jesus as the shining example who let go of everything—status, respect, reputation, wealth, time, space, cleanliness, tidiness, oversight, authority, power, predictability, what he had always done, where he always sat—and went on an adventure. He swapped all those things for messiness, dirt, betrayal, unpredictability, cost, pain, isolation, vulnerability, puzzlement, despair, suffering and danger, right through to death itself. But look at the payback! This was the only way to turn heaven and earth upside down and kick off the new age of the kingdom, where everyone and anyone can get a glimpse of how glorious Jesus really is and start to help put things right. We can do no better than worship our vindicated, resurrected, successful gold-medal Jesus.

So you need to work out, in God's economy, how you can help. God doesn't *need* you but he *wants* you to help, and he's chosen you (yes, you!) and will work in you from the inside out to bring you up to speed for the job he's given you—but it's always your choice.

We want Messy Church leaders to be shining examples of living as a Christian today. So keep an eye on the little things. Cut out the muttering, grumbling and backbiting. In your life at home, school and/or work, and in your free time, keep a check on yourselves and deliberately imagine that glowing sanctuary light shining out through you to bring hope and love wherever you go. Dear friends, we're in this together. We are awed by the work you do and the work God's doing through you. We take our hats off to your imagination, creativity, hospitality, courage, energy and sheer joy in serving God through serving others. High five, Messy people!

You know what an amazing team we have at BRF— we do our best to support you and love to hear your stories and find out what God is doing through you. There's Jane, for example, cheering on the Regional Coordinators; Martyn visiting Messy Churches all over the country and bringing two-way encouragement and inspiration; and me making and keeping Messy friends all over the world. Bear with us when we get it wrong and don't serve you as we should—we are trying our best, but we, like you, are making it up as we go along and need your forbearance!

More than anything, dear Messy friends, *enjoy* this ministry God's given us! *Celebrate* the way so many ordinary, unexpected people are finding the love of God through your Messy Church. Make a note of God at work and praise him for it! I know we've said it before, but saying it again reminds us as well as you how much there is to be gleeful about, how much to give thanks for. Party, my friends, party!

I suppose we could be proud of this work: nearly 3000 new congregations in ten years; a team of 80 Regional Coordinators; maybe 14,000 new people coming to church; Messy Church in 20 countries; perhaps the biggest multi-denominational mission agency of today… This number-crunching is fun, but hollow because we know what we're really proud of is the way Jesus is being made known to and loved

by more and more people. He is the one who has made all this happen, not us, and if it was all stripped away, if Messy Church was dissolved tomorrow, that would still leave each of us loving, trusting and hoping in Jesus for our present and our future. What matters is him at work in us, loving and transforming us, dragging our reluctant lives from atrophy to power and purpose. If there were no more Messy Church, we would still be focused on Jesus and the awesome rescue plan of God through his death and resurrection.

There's still so much to do—God's 'home improvements' inside us and in our Messy work, building the kingdom in our communities. Despite many past mistakes and inadvertently wobbly foundations, in God's wonderful construction zone we can let go of the past, trusting it all to him, and joyfully get on with the present with a clear vision of how fantastic the finished building will be. We are all just trying to live up to the reality of the cosmic destruction and construction God's done in us already.

Stick to the Messy values! They're kingdom ones. And learn from each other—go and spend time with other Messy leaders and check out what they do well. We all get upset by people who can't see the bigger picture, who try to drag things back to traditions, power bases and regulations, and who lack generosity of spirit—and we wheel out clever arguments that get us nowhere. But we don't need to get defensive. We can relax, sure that we're kingdom-building and that ultimately Jesus will do away with every human power base and simply pulse through everyone and everything, like a tablet being charged, connected to the internet and suddenly capable of phenomenal achievements. Stick with the big picture through the ordinary little decisions, dear Messy friends! It's going Godwards, even when it feels as if it's standing still.

Check out your relationships. If anybody's got the hump, fall over yourself to sort it out. Forget everything—your pride, your hurt, your knowledge that you are right(!)—and be a peacemaker, so you can celebrate on every occasion! Rejoice each time you think about what God is doing. Gloat with friends over what Jesus is doing: be gleeful, thankful, bewildered, awestruck, humbled, amazed, encouraged and dumbstruck, and turn it all into praise—not of yourselves, of course! Not of Messy

Church, of course! Praise of Jesus Christ and his generosity in doing all this through (and despite) you and us. We are living in the overlap between two ages. Jesus is around every corner, so live life lightly; don't get stressed or weighed down with worries, but give everything over to him in a spirit of thankfulness. And you will find yourselves living in an unshakeable peace that goes way beyond common sense.

To help Jesus keep you in this wonderful state of trust and hope, do your bit. Focus intentionally on the hidden reality of the kingdom; look out for God at work in messy people and in the messiness of life. Deliberately notice and comment on what is true, admirable, positive, glorious, funny, moving, life-affirming, surprising, inspiring or just plain good. Reflect on it. Don't let it pass you by. Let God change you, your outlook and your expectations and stretch you into a different shape. That way you'll find him in so many people and places!

We are so grateful to those of you who show your support with gifts of money to BRF. We thank God for you. We try not to stress about how this ministry will be paid for year by year and trust in God's provision, but it's such an encouragement to us that you care enough to give towards it: that symbol of love and solidarity means so much. There are few churches giving to BRF's Messy ministry as yet, so we are humbled and delighted by the ones who have seen the need and jumped at the chance to meet it. Part of the reason we love to receive gifts is because it trumps those who say, 'Messy Church can't be financially self-sustaining and so it doesn't count.' Your generosity reflects well on the whole network, even those who have no way of contributing yet. Your money is a huge and godly thing—a sacrament that says far more than its concrete reality. In God's weird and wonderful economy we know you'll find all *your* needs are met, because God's hands are always open and ready to give, give, give—especially in his gift that keeps on giving: Jesus.

So say hello to your Messy team from us and give them our love. We pray and know that the grace of our Lord Jesus Christ will be with you and your Messy families. Bless you.

MESSY JOURNEYS

Not long ago, Martyn Payne was leading a training morning in South London to introduce a number of congregational leaders to Messy Church. As always, there were all sorts of stories shared, both by those who were already on a messy journey at their church and by others who were keen to reach out to their local community by starting a Messy Church of their own. Among those who came was Natalie, who had an inspiring story to share. Here is that story in her words.

'MESSY CHURCH CHANGED OUR LIVES!'

Natalie Scott

I first attended a Messy Church at Caterham Community Church, in Surrey. I was completely wowed by how welcoming and friendly the experience was and my children absolutely loved it. It was organised chaos, but it was like walking into heaven. It was also amazing that my family could spend time with their father, as he is always at work.

I started to attend the sessions more regularly and found myself becoming more and more interested in the whole Christian story. My children began to ask questions and I felt I wanted to answer them in a way that was connected to God, so I needed to know those answers first! I completed a Christianity Explored course and then an Alpha course at different locations, and now we go as a family to St Mary's, Caterham, where I have been confirmed and my children baptised.

We are hoping that St Mary's will be able to start a Messy Church so that many other young families can enjoy an experience such as ours in a relaxed, crazy, messy environment.

Many thanks to Messy Church for changing our lives!

The Great Big BRF Mess-About!

We've always been aware of the danger of settling into a routine—human beings are hardwired to require rhythm AND change, hence the need for religious festivals to break up the more humdrum year of daily faith observance. If it's all rhythm and no highlights, we run the risk of losing our energy, failing to engage our imagination and assuming we can never change anything. We can end up like Pooh and Piglet, going round and round the tree hunting the Heffalump. Also, as Messy Church takes a lot of effort to organise, we may end up firmly set in an inescapable rut.

If you feel your Messy Church team needs a boost, here's a fun and easy-to-arrange idea to avoid falling into the humdrum Heffalump trap. Why not join in **The Great Big BRF Mess-About**? It's very simple: you take your team to visit another Messy Church!

Why? Because visiting someone else's Messy Church will give your team fresh energy. Either it will be an awesomely fantastic Messy Church, in which case you will come away with tons of their ideas to make yours better, or it will be less successful and you will come home appreciating all the good people and things in yours that you had previously taken for granted. Then again, it could (most likely) be very similar to yours but with a few interesting differences you can learn from, and you will meet lovely people to make friends with, be encouraged by, share resources with and pray for over the coming months as you feel united in God's mission in your area.

You might also find it's very helpful to feel what it's like to be a stranger coming into a new community where you're not in charge! The sense of being a guest will provide insights into how families feel coming to your Messy Church.

Also, as you'll see, there's a simple thankyou card to fill in and send to your host church, which will help your team reflect on the experience and should be greatly encouraging to the host church.

Of course we can ring up another local church *any* time and invite ourselves to visit, but sometimes we need an *excuse* to make the effort to visit another local Messy Church or to invite other churches to ours: we might have good intentions, but we're so busy with our own Messiness that the months go by and that visit just never happens.

So here are some helpful resources. Don't forget to invite other people to your Messy Church, too!

- The **Directory** will show you your nearest Messy Churches and give you the contact details.
- The **invitation** can be customised, printed off or downloaded for emailing or use on your website.
- The **thankyou card** can be used to give positive feedback to your hosts.
- Your **Regional Coordinator** may be able to link you with another good Messy Church.

www.messychurch.org.uk/bigmessabout

RESOURCING TEAM DISCIPLESHIP

MESSY CHURCH CONFERENCE

CELEBRATING AND LEARNING WITH THE WORLDWIDE FAMILY OF MESSY CHURCH

An amazing, life-changing opportunity to meet Messy friends from all over the world, the Messy Church Conference is 16–18 May this year in Hertfordshire. We'd love you all to come to make the most of this unique opportunity for training, equipping and encouragement with guests from at least three continents. The whole BRF Messy Church team will be there and we're looking forward to seeing you again, or meeting you for the first time, and having lots of quality time with you! Canon Dr George Lings will be giving challenging, brain-stretching and inspirational input, and we'll be getting very Messy... If you help lead your Messy Church, why not ask your church if they would help with the cost? Day tickets are available for the 17th. Details at **www.messychurch. org.uk/event/messy-church-conference**

Messy CHURCH **16-18 May 2016**
Conference 2016
@ HIGH LEIGH CONFERENCE CENTRE, HODDESDON, HERTS, UK (30 MINUTES BY TRAIN FROM LONDON)

FEATURING GEORGE LINGS KEYNOTE SPEAKER & FISCHY MUSIC

Growing Messy Leaders

We're delighted to be working with the experienced team at CPAS to offer Growing Messy Leaders days. These revolutionary training days for your team are to make the most of the opportunities for growing leaders within your Messy Church. They're for all ages from nine upwards (under-16s must be accompanied)—a real multigenerational experience! They help us look outwards, to the work we are doing and the people we're doing it with, and inwards/upwards, to our relationship with Christ, the cornerstone of the work. And they're huge fun. Keep an eye on the Events page of the website to see if there's one near you, or ask your diocesan/ district missioners, lay training coordinators or bishops if your denomination could host one. If you could offer your church and team to host it, they will probably be thrilled! Contact messychurch@brf.org.uk or 01235 858246 for full details of cost and availability.

GROWING MESSY LEADERS

Time:

At:

Cost:

Lunch:

To book:

CPAS brings their extensive experience of growing leaders in churches to help Messy Churches.

BRF's Messy Church team and CPAS are working together to help Messy Church team members and leaders of all ages become better leaders through team-building work and leadership theory and reflective practice.

Whether you're nine or 99, these hands-on, fun, fast-moving and action-packed training days will give you the opportunity to understand more of the practicalities of leading a Messy Church, develop your teamwork and reflect on your inner relationship with God and those around you.

Take your Messy team to a different level. Come as a team! Bring your leaders young and old to this fun, inspirational, useful and paradigm-shifting all-age training day.

All young people (9–16 year olds) must be accompanied by a responsible adult. This training day will also be helpful for those in other forms of team ministry and lay leadership but is focused clearly on Messy Church.

DID YOU KNOW? WE ARE ON PINTEREST!

PINTEREST.COM/ MESSYCHURCHBRF

MESSY MONASTIC

George Lings

What on earth could Messy Church have in common with the monastic tradition? Bustle and buzz, fun and food, and paint and glue seem miles away from celibate monks, hushed cloisters and ethereal music.

What they have in common is the instinct that it takes a number of different spaces in order to fully express communal life in Christ and to live more fully as human beings. Both streams challenge the idea that being church is adequately expressed mainly or only through attending public worship.

When Lucy Moore started the first Messy Church in Portsmouth over a decade ago, she built upon several values. I'd put them this way. Church is a Jesus-centred community in which people deserve a true welcome, everyone has a level of creativity, families matter, leadership is shared, worship works best when it draws on the rest of life, and meals offer hospitality, which fosters community. I think she intuitively knew that you can't get all those things either out of, much less into, an act of worship. The bit that is called 'worship' is just one contributory factor.

For some years I have been studying a whole range of monastic communities: some from 1500 years ago, others just clocking up a decade or two. Some were gathered and others dispersed. Some were for singles only, others have married members. The harder I looked and the more I read their guiding documents, the more I kept seeing a set of seven spaces with functions they all seemed to need. Here they are in reverse alphabetical order with a note on what each is for. See if you can spot the Messy Church match or overlap.

- *Scriptorium* Here Bibles, prayer books and wise writings were lovingly copied by hand, to be passed on to the next generation and help start yet more monasteries.
- *Refectory* In this room the community was nourished and fed, as were its guests as the monasteries became the early hotel system of Western Europe.
- *Garden* Gardening helped keep people fit and staved off idleness. The garden was the source of food for the community.
- *Cloister* This square colonnade joins up the other places. Planned and surprise meetings occur there, both of which are part of community life. Handling both well, in humility, matters.
- *Chapter* Here part of the guiding document was read out. Then decisions were taken, but the leader was consulted before acting on them.
- *Chapel* Public prayer is the function of this room, which took the pattern of a number of short services during the day.
- *Cell* This is the one private space for each person to be alone with God in prayer and slow, careful reading. Some sources call it the place where God teaches us the most.

My understanding is that, throughout Christian history, God has raised up the monastic tradition to show all Christians what a fuller life in Christ looks like. Put in

Garden

Scriptorium

Refectory

Cloister

other language, if you want to follow Jesus' way of travelling closely, then it is a whole-life business. It cannot be done just through better church services. Church is more than the 'chapel' function.

That's exactly the same with Messy Church. Healthy ones know that life is about work, rest and play. Part of the mess is that there are lots of elements. Life in Christ is neither simple nor singular. Some monastics taught that the *opus Dei*—the work of God—was made of prayer, study and manual work.

How do you know if your Messy Church is making progress? I really doubt that the measure to use is whether the celebration goes on longer. How about other factors such as the depth of welcome, the release of creativity, the building of family life, the empowering of leaders, and generous hospitality, as well as worship, the quality of which is fed by all the other elements? In short, is your Messy Church using all its diverse spaces so that its community looks more like Jesus and is drawing others to Jesus?

I think Messy Church has real overlaps with this monastic insight into healthy community life in Christ. Messy Church is right to insist that each element matters and that only when all elements are working together do you get a healthy expression of church. It's time to get out of the mentality of chapel being all that really counts and into the other places—knowing they are all elements of being church. Of course worship is important and it should guard the other

places. One picture of the interrelationship is that some call chapel the 'heart' of community, chapter the 'head' and refectory the 'stomach'. Each needs the others.

There's the surprise. Messy Church has real overlaps with the long tradition of monasticism. Any Messy Church could study the seven spaces and work out which were strongly present and where there might be issues—such as how you do cell in overall Messy Church life. I'm glad of the overlap and that both are holding out a richer way to be church to the rest of the Church.

If you would like to know more, there is a Church Army's Research Unit booklet entitled 'Seven Sacred Spaces: Expressing community life in Christ' (*Encounters on the Edge no. 43*) available as a pdf from **www.encountersontheedge.org.uk**.

I hope to meet some of you at the Messy Church Conference in May 2016 and hear how your range of spaces is developing.

George Lings was an Anglican vicar for 21 years. Since 1997 he has worked for Church Army, directing its research unit, and he has spoken about fresh expressions of church around the developed world. He wrote large parts of 'Mission-shaped Church', the 2004 Church of England report on fresh expressions of church. He became a Canon of Sheffield Cathedral in 2011 and is a Vice-President trustee of BRF.

Cell

Chapter

Chapel

A day in the life of...
ROBERT FERRIS
REPUBLIC OF IRELAND REGIONAL COORDINATOR

A couple of times when I've been on the phone to a UK call centre and given my address, the reply has come back, 'Seriously? You live there? Does it exist?'—and I have assured the call centre worker that, yes, there is indeed a village in County Cork called Blarney and, yes, it's the place of the famous stone. I've been the Church of Ireland (Anglican) minister in Blarney since 2012 and, to top it off, I was appointed on *1 April*!

When I first arrived in Blarney, I discovered Messy Church, which has been running since 2008. We have a great team, which we are continuing to develop. Two years ago Jane Leadbetter asked if I would take on the role of Regional Coordinator, and I must say I am loving the adventure that is helping all sorts of churches around the country grapple with mission in their particular contexts. Many of the Republic of Ireland churches running Messy Church are small, traditional congregations who are discovering

that they have on their doorsteps families who are not engaging with church in other ways.

As Regional Coordinator, I work closely with Jill Hamilton, the Regional Coordinator for Northern Ireland. I have also met with people in all sorts of places: I've been to our theological college and Liturgical Committee; to Messy Meet-ups in Dublin and Cork, Round Table discussions in England and General Synod; and I'm really looking forward to meeting up with the Messy family at the Messy Church Conference later this year.

The rate of growth of Messy Church in Ireland is fantastic. From the last count I reckon about ten per cent of Church of Ireland churches have some sort of Messy Church programme, and I'm aware of another five or six churches considering it. Within the Irish context, Messy Church seems to work really well when the parish or congregation decides it is up for doing something different. It takes two or three key people to say, 'Let's give it a go!' Can Messy Church thrive in a traditional parish context? Yes, and it can lead to wider community engagement. Why not give it a go? More information can be found on our website **messyireland.blogspot.com** or **facebook.com/messyireland**.

YOUTH COLUMN

Daniel Robins

My name is Daniel Robins. I'm 14 and I joined St Editha's (The Church on The Green, in Amington, Tamworth, Staffordshire) four years ago with my family. I love it there, and one of my favourite parts about it is the Messy Church that started just after we arrived.

I join in with the activities as normal in the craft time (although I often make examples for people who lead the activity beforehand) and thoroughly enjoy them. However, as people are sitting

down for the celebration time, I play the Messy Church theme song on my tenor horn, and then help out with the puppets that are often part of the celebration. Sometimes I change the slides being projected on to the screen, and I am part of drama sketches too.

When I became a teenager, my birthday fell on a Messy Church day. My mum said we wouldn't be going because of that, but I made sure we did, knowing it would make it extra-special! I did, however, take advantage of my situation by requesting hot dogs for the meal—sausages are my favourite food by far!

I love Messy Church so much because, quite simply, it's so fun. I wouldn't normally get to do some of the stuff there, especially the food crafts. I wish it took place every day rather than every six weeks!

You can make a difference...

Messy Church has already had an enormous impact on thousands of people, many of whom wouldn't have otherwise engaged with their local church. We want to enable many more people to be blessed by this ministry, both now and also well into the future. Please would you and/or your church prayerfully consider whether you could support Lucy and her team's ministry with a one-off gift or—even better—with a regular commitment? Whether you can give £5, £10, £50, £100 or more, every single pound counts!

For further information about making a gift to BRF or to discuss how a specific donation could be used to develop BRF's Messy Church ministry, please contact Sophie Aldred (Head of Fundraising) or Richard Fisher (Chief Executive) by email at **fundraising@brf.org.uk** or by phone on 01865 319700.

Parts of the BRF whole

Richard Fisher

A few years ago I was talking to a church minister. He told me that he knew all about The Bible Reading Fellowship (BRF): 'You're the publisher of those Bible reading notes, aren't you?' I replied that there was a little bit more to BRF than that and told him about the various strands of BRF's work. I loved his response: 'I never realised there was so much there. It's like an Aladdin's Cave!'

Perhaps you're looking for something to inspire you or challenge you afresh in your own journey of faith? Perhaps you'd like something that would help to reinvigorate your regular Bible reading and prayer times? Maybe you're a primary school teacher and would appreciate ideas and resources to explore Christianity in the classroom? Or a parent or children's leader in church looking for help and inspiration as you explore the Bible and Christian faith with your children? Or perhaps you're wondering how your church could engage with more people in your local community?

So what would you find in our Aladdin's Cave today?

You'd find books, ebooks, Bible reading notes and other resources to help you—whatever age or stage you're at in your journey of life and faith—to grow in your Christian faith and your understanding of the Bible, prayer and discipleship. There's also inspiration, ideas, resources and support to help you and your church engage with your local community through Messy Church, Who Let The Dads Out? and The Gift of Years, all of which are part of BRF. There are creative, imaginative programmes, resources and training available to help primary school teachers and their pupils explore Christianity creatively. And there are resources, ideas and inspiration for anyone involved in children's and family ministry in their church.

At BRF we're passionate about seeing lives and communities transformed through the Christian faith. Every month we touch the lives of thousands of people of all ages throughout the UK and in other countries through our resources and programmes.

In subsequent issues of *Get Messy!* we're going to introduce and feature some of the different aspects of BRF's work and the people involved. But in the meantime, why not come over to **www.brf.org.uk** and explore our Aladdin's Cave for yourself? You might be

Reprinted with permission from **Get Messy! Jan–Apr 2016**, published by Messy Church, a part of BRF

SESSION MATERIAL: JANUARY

MESSY REFLECTION

SIAN ASHFORD

In Jerusalem lived a man named Simeon who was a good man and godly. He was waiting for the time when God would take away Israel's sorrow, and the Holy Spirit was in him. Simeon had been told by the Holy Spirit that he would not die before he saw the Christ promised by the Lord. The Spirit led Simeon to the Temple. When Mary and Joseph brought the baby Jesus to the Temple to do what the law said they must do, Simeon took the baby in his arms and thanked God:

'Now, Lord, you can let me, your servant,
     die in peace as you said.
With my own eyes I have seen your salvation,
which you prepared before all people.
It is a light for the non-Jewish people to see
     and an honour for your people, the Israelites.'

Jesus' father and mother were amazed at what Simeon had said about him. Then Simeon blessed them and said to Mary, 'God has chosen this child to cause the fall and rise of many in Israel. He will be a sign from God that many people will not accept so that the thoughts of many will be made known. And the things that will happen will make your heart sad, too.'
     There was a prophetess, Anna, from the family of Phanuel in the tribe of Asher. Anna was very old. She had once been married for seven years. Then her husband died, and she was a widow for eighty-four years. Anna never left the Temple but worshipped God, going without food and praying day and night. Standing there at that time, she thanked God and spoke about Jesus to all who were waiting for God to free Jerusalem.
Luke 2:25–38 (NCV)

What an amazing experience this must have been for Mary and Joseph. They took their baby boy to the Temple, as was customary, and were met by two wonderful, wise and godly people who had been waiting for them their whole lives.

Simeon and Anna were chosen very carefully by God to prophesy over Jesus. As elderly members of the Jewish community, they would have been well respected and their prophecies would have been taken seriously. God also very deliberately chose both a male and a female prophet to emphasise that all can welcome Jesus as Saviour.

The Holy Spirit had told Simeon long ago that he would not die before he saw the Christ. Simeon held on to this promise and waited patiently, fully expecting God to stand by his word. He would have been striving to find his Saviour in every baby he saw, so that he could die in peace. His example to us is one of perseverance and dedication: Simeon spent years looking for Jesus and he found him. His story challenges us to look at our own lives and ask if we are looking for the Saviour of the world with the same perseverance and dedication.

Anna was a widow who had lived in the Temple most of her long life, committing herself to the Lord. She recognised Jesus straight away and rejoiced with thanksgiving for the boy who would save the world. Anna couldn't contain her excitement at having met her Saviour. The Bible extract above says she 'spoke about Jesus to all who were waiting for God to free Jerusalem' (v. 38). Are we so excited about Jesus that we can't help telling everyone we meet about him? As you meet with your Messy Church congregation this week, consider ways to tell them the exciting news about Jesus the Saviour of the world.

MEALTIME CARDS

- How easy do you find it to wait for things?
- What are the best and worst things about getting older?
- Who is the wisest person you know?

TAKE-HOME IDEA

Ask an older person—maybe a grandparent, a great-grandparent or an older neighbour—to tell you some stories about what life was like when they were children. Perhaps you could turn their stories into a book!

You might like to say this prayer together at home:

Thank you, God, that however old we are we will always be your children. Help us to see our older people as you see them, and to be thankful for all they have to share with us. In Jesus' name, Amen

DOWNLOAD

Go to www.messychurch.org.uk/extra-resources/ to download all templates at A4 size, including a session planning sheet

 MessyChurchBRF   MessyChurchBRF @MessyChurchBRF

PAST, PRESENT AND FUTURE BY DEBBIE PEATMAN

2

6

8

MESSY HEALTH CHECK

As you consider discipleship, are there any families or individuals in whom you can see God at work? What next step might they need? How is your own discipleship going?

HOW DOES THIS SESSION HELP PEOPLE GROW IN CHRIST?

The importance of different age groups learning, playing and worshipping together is one of Messy Church's core values. Today's story offers an opportunity to celebrate our old people, so often overlooked in today's society. When Jesus was brought as a baby to the Temple to be dedicated, it was an old man, Simeon, and an old woman, Anna, who had the insight to recognise him as the promised Messiah. Full of joy, they prophesied his future and told others about him. Older people still have gifts of insight, wisdom and encouragement essential to the health and balance of our Messy communities. Today's session is about valuing, drawing out and sharing those gifts.

BIBLE REFERENCE

Luke 2:25–38

MESSY TEAM THEME

- Does our Messy Church offer a real welcome to older people as themselves, or simply as carers for the children?
- How can we encourage interaction between the generations?
- What was it about Simeon and Anna that enabled them to see who Jesus really was?

10

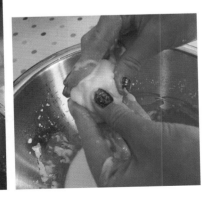

SESSION MATERIAL: JANUARY

ACTIVITIES

1. SIMEON'S PRAYER

You will need: template printed on to card; light-themed stickers, pictures, sequins, etc; glue

Decorate the edge of your card to make a shiny frame for Simeon's prayer.

Talk about why Simeon might have described baby Jesus as being a 'light' for the world.

2. WE HAVE HISTORY!

You will need: long strip of wallpaper; pencil; pictures representing events or fashions from each decade of the last 100 years; glue sticks; A7 pieces of plain paper; felt pens

Draw dividing lines on your wallpaper to make ten sections, each representing a decade. Label the sections from left to right, starting with '1920s' and ending with '2010s'. Invite people to stick the pictures where they think they should go, then draw themselves on an A7 piece of paper and stick this on the decade in which they were born.

Talk about how many different decades we were born in, and what a lot of history we've seen between us.

3. HOW WILL I LOOK?

You will need: someone who can make up faces to look older (try asking around local drama groups or theatres—they are often delighted to help and it's a great way to make community connections. Failing that, a team member armed with some make-up and a YouTube tutorial could do the job!); mirror

Spend a little time looking at your new face in the mirror.

Talk about how it feels to see your face looking older. How else do you think your body might change as you age?

4. GUESS WHO?

You will need: numbered photos of team members as babies or children; named photos of them as they are now; pens; paper

See if you can work out who is who! (This has the added benefit of reinforcing knowledge of team members' identities and names.)

Talk about how people have changed, and how they are still the same.

5. TANGLED!

You will need: several heaps of tangled wool, ribbon or string

Work together with family members or friends to try to untangle one of the heaps. Will you be patient enough to get to the end?

Talk about how hard it is to be patient when something takes a long time to complete. Talk about how today's story is all about two old people who waited their whole lives for a promise to come true.

6. BABY IN ICE

You will need: paper cups; water; jelly babies; freezer space; washing-up bowls; warm gloves (waterproof if possible)

(NB: check jelly baby packaging to ensure there are no traces of nuts)

Before the session fill each paper cup with water to a depth of about 2 cm, then freeze. When it is solid, wet a jelly baby and hold it on top of the ice for few minutes (this stops it sliding to one side.) Cover with a further 2 cm of water and refreeze. Start all this 24 hours before Messy Church.

Wearing gloves and working over a washing-up bowl, peel off your paper cup, then see if you can free your baby from the ice without damaging him!

Talk about Simeon and Anna's patience as they waited a long time to welcome a very special baby.

7. SHARING SKILLS

You will need: some older people who are prepared to teach simple, 'old-fashioned'

MessyChurchBRF   **MessyChurchBRF**   **@MessyChurchBRF**

skills such as knitting, polishing silver, wood whittling, etc.; necessary materials

Offer a masterclass in some traditional skills!

Talk about how much different generations can learn from each other. Could any of the young people offer to teach the older people some 'modern-day' skills suh as how to use a mobile phone, or loom-band art, at a future Messy Church?

8. SIMEON AND ANNA FACES

You will need: paper plates; selection of fruit slices (e.g. apple, kiwi fruit, pineapple); orange segments; raisins and other dried fruits; cans of 'squirty' cream

(NB: check cream packaging to ensure there are no traces of nuts)

Make the face of an old man or lady with fruit on your paper plate, then squirt on lots of white hair!

Talk about why old people often have white hair. What colour is your hair?

9. LIGHTING-UP PRAYERS

You will need: sandpit; tea lights; matches; tapers; bucket of water

A candle is hard and cold until we light it; then it becomes a living flame. Light your candle, put it in the sandpit and watch the flame for a little while. Ask God to help you see how things that look lifeless can come alive if we light them up.

(NB: light candles for small children and carefully supervise them. Have a bucket of water nearby just in case.)

Talk about how the old people in today's story had spent their whole lives praying. That meant they were able to recognise Jesus as the light of the world.

10. TWO THINGS AT ONCE!

You will need: large bowl or deep tray; spoons; cornflour; water

Put some cornflour in the bowl or tray and slowly add water up to about half the amount of cornflour. Let everyone help you stir it. What emerges will be a substance that is both a liquid and a solid—brilliant for messy moulding, pouring and playing.

Talk about whether what you've made is a liquid or a solid, or both. Jesus was an ordinary baby, but Simeon and Anna could see that he was also God—two things at once!

CELEBRATION

You will need: simple nativity set; two cloaks or shawls; two walking sticks; someone primed to read

Explain that you will need some help to tell today's story, and get two volunteers to be Simeon and Anna. Give each a cloak and a walking stick. Get them to practise moving as if they're very old.

Our story begins with this little family. *(Indicate the nativity set.)* Who can tell me who they are? Last month we remembered the story of Jesus being born at Christmas, but all these people didn't stay in the stable for ever, did they? The shepherds went back to their fields. Once the wise men had visited, they went back to their home in the East. *(Remove the wise men and shepherds from the scene.)* But what about Mary and Joseph and their baby? Where did they go? Today, we're going to hear about one of the very first journeys they made with Jesus when he was still a tiny baby. *(Lift them out of the stable.)* Who'd like to come and hold them for us?

Mary and Joseph set out with Jesus to go to a special place to say thank you to God for him. Does anybody know where they went to say that thank you? Sometimes, people bring their babies to church to say thank you to God. Well, Mary and Joseph took Jesus to their holy place, which was called the Temple.

Now we know Jesus was a very special baby, but do you think he looked special? No, I'm pretty sure he looked just like any other baby. So when they came into the Temple, there were lots of people about, but they didn't notice anything unusual about Jesus. Even the priest didn't notice anything different—he thought this baby looked just like all the others. When Mary and Joseph had said their prayers, they almost slipped away without anyone taking any notice of them at all. But then, all of a sudden, someone did notice them. A very old man appeared out of the shadows. Simeon, our old man—are you there? He jumped up out of his seat—even though he was too old to jump—and he came running up to them—even though he was too old to run! They didn't know what to think! And this is what he said.

Reader: 'Lord, at last I can die in peace when my time comes! Now, with my own eyes, I've seen how you're going to save us. Here he is, for the whole world to see—the pride of his own people, and a light for every nation on earth.'

Well, that was quite a surprise for Mary and Joseph, but what Simeon said next gave Mary even more to think about.

Reader: 'Mary, your son is no ordinary little boy. He's going to turn the whole country upside down. He's going to be unpopular with a lot of people, because he's going to bring a lot of things into the open that people would rather keep hidden. And—I'm sorry to tell you this, Mary—he's going to break your heart.'

Now that was strange enough, but then, all of a sudden, an old woman came running up to join them. Anna, are you there? She was very old and very creaky, but she managed to run over to them all the same. She was so excited! She burst into a song of praise to God, and then she went off telling everyone the Saviour had arrived. Thank you, Simeon and Anna!

I wonder what it was about Simeon and Anna that meant they could see what nobody else could see. Well, for one thing they had spent their whole lives praying—talking to God and listening to God. Because they had learned how to listen to God and spent so much time with him, they could see things other people didn't notice. They could understand things other people were too busy to think about. They weren't young, they weren't beautiful, and they weren't clever or important, but they were wise. They saw what no one else noticed that day—that this baby was very special indeed.

Our world is moving and changing so fast that it can be hard for older people to keep up. They probably don't understand the latest technology or follow the latest fashions, and sometimes we might think that means they've got nothing important to offer. But we couldn't be more wrong! There are some gifts—such as patience, wisdom and insight—that take years to grow. Without our older people, we'd lose some of the most precious treasure in our communities.

Simeon and Anna were the wisest people in the whole Temple. As we remember them today, let's thank God for the gifts our own older members bring to Messy Church and celebrate all we can learn from them.

PRAYER

Thank you, Lord, for the patience, wisdom and insight of Simeon and Anna. Thank you for our own older members who can help to grow those gifts in our Messy community. Help us all to love and value one another, and to see beneath the surface of people to the truth that you see inside them. In Jesus' name, Amen

SONG SUGGESTIONS

'Not'—Kay Morgan-Gurr and Steve Morgan-Gurr (Song Solutions Daybreak)

'Man looks on the outside'—Nigel Hemming (Vineyard Songs)

MEAL SUGGESTION

Beef pastry pie, green beans and carrots, followed by sponge pudding and custard

SESSION MATERIAL: FEBRUARY
THE LAST SUPPER BY PETE MAIDMENT

MESSY REFLECTION

DEBBIE PEATMAN

On the first day of the Festival of Unleavened Bread the disciples came to Jesus and asked him, 'Where do you want us to get the Passover meal ready for you?'

'Go to a certain man in the city,' he said to them, 'and tell him: "The Teacher says, My hour has come; my disciples and I will celebrate the Passover at your house."'

The disciples did as Jesus had told them and prepared the Passover meal.

When it was evening, Jesus and the twelve disciples sat down to eat. During the meal Jesus said, 'I tell you, one of you will betray me.'

The disciples were very upset and began to ask him, one after the other, 'Surely, Lord, you don't mean me?'

Jesus answered, 'One who dips his bread in the dish with me will betray me. The Son of Man will die as the Scriptures say he will, but how terrible for that man who will betray the Son of Man! It would have been better for that man if he had never been born!'

Judas, the traitor, spoke up. 'Surely, Teacher, you don't mean me?' he asked.

Jesus answered, 'So you say.'

While they were eating, Jesus took a piece of bread, gave a prayer of thanks, broke it, and gave it to his disciples. 'Take and eat it,' he said; 'this is my body.'

Then he took a cup, gave thanks to God, and gave it to them. 'Drink it, all of you,' he said; 'this is my blood, which seals God's covenant, my blood poured out for many for the forgiveness of sins. I tell you, I will never again drink this wine until the day I drink the new wine with you in my Father's Kingdom.'

Then they sang a hymn and went out to the Mount of Olives.

Matthew 26:17–30 (GNT)

Stories don't come much messier than that of Jesus' last supper with his disciples. The venue is uncertain until the last minute and preparations are rushed. As they gather around the table, their relationships are in a mess, what with Jesus' talk of betrayal, the whole group in confusion, and Judas in denial. Worst of all, Jesus seems intent on talking about his own death. All this at the Passover meal, which is supposed to be the most joyful event of the year. What a mess!

In the midst of it all, Jesus takes two key elements of the meal—bread and wine—and uses them to create a picture of what is going on and a sign for his friends to remember. The bread Jesus has shared with his betrayer is broken as a picture of what is about to happen to his own body. The poured-out wine, a picture of his poured-out blood, is shared as a sign of forgiveness. It's a messy, transient picture—eaten and drunk, disappearing like a child's work of art, leaving crumbs and splashes behind. Yet, out of the mess, Jesus shows us the way to be mended; out of something as transient as a meal, he gives us a gift of eternal significance.

Is it appropriate to share Holy Communion in Messy Church? Concern is sometimes expressed as to whether or not a Messy gathering can possibly be reverent or serious enough for this sort of worship. Many denominations, after all, have hedged Communion around with rules and regulations that prevent children or those on the messy edges from taking part. And yet I can't help thinking that Messy Church might just be the perfect place to receive, explore and celebrate the messy sacrament Jesus made for us in bread and wine.

MEALTIME CARDS

- What's the best meal you've ever eaten?
- How does sitting down to a family meal make you feel?
- What else could we do together to remember what Jesus has done for us?

TAKE-HOME IDEA

Why not make a commitment to eat around the table together at least once a week; to turn the TV off and ask each other to share one thing that has gone well recently and one thing that has been difficult. Use this discussion as a chance to pray for each other. Do an internet search for 'examen' if you want more ideas on this kind of prayer!

Dear Jesus, when we remember what you did for us, we can't help but be grateful. Help us to remember your sacrifice each day, and to have the courage to do what we can for other people. Amen

SESSION MATERIAL: FEBRUARY

1

6

7

> ## MESSY HEALTH CHECK
> How are you encouraging generosity in your Messy Church team? And in your families?

HOW DOES THIS SESSION HELP PEOPLE GROW IN CHRIST?

As families we do all sorts of different things together that are 'our thing'. No doubt we can all think of dozens of traditions, big or small, that mark us out as us. In the Church we have a few similar activities, and the sharing of bread and wine is one of those incredibly important reminders of who we are. By sharing in the story of the Last Supper, and partaking in the activity that Christ called us to remember him by, we grow deeper into God's family and, as we grow together, we also grow up into God. Remembering Christ's sacrifice helps us grow in gratitude to him and in relationship with the God who created us.

BIBLE REFERENCE
Matthew 26:17–30

MESSY TEAM THEME
- What goes through your mind as you approach the Communion table to share in Jesus' special meal?
- What other activities can we do together to remind us of the special link we all share?

ACTIVITIES

1. TASTY FLATBREAD

You will need: wholemeal flour; jug of water; mixing bowls; rolling pins; scales; clean surface for rolling; non-stick frying pans; small camping stoves (the ones that use gas cartridges are perfect); paper plates; pens; butter or jam (optional); round-ended knives and spoons (optional)

(NB: check flour packaging to ensure there are no traces of nuts)

Mix together 450 g plain wholemeal flour and 250 ml water to make a good firm bread dough. Encourage people to roll a golf-ball-sized dough sphere on a floured surface into a thin flatbread no more than 2–3

Reprinted with permission from **Get Messy! Jan–Apr 2016**, published by Messy Church, a part of BRF

THE LAST SUPPER BY PETE MAIDMENT

mm thick. Ask adults and children old enough to be responsible to heat a dry frying pan over a portable gas stove and cook the flatbread for 20–30 seconds on each side. Once it has cooled a little (leave on named plates while this happens), invite people to either eat it as it is or spread with a little butter and/or jam.

Talk about the last time you baked. How does the aroma of bread cooking make you feel? Why do you think Jesus used bread as a way for his disciples to remember him?

2. SQUASHY GRAPES

You will need: red grapes; sieves; bowls; disposable plastic gloves; beakers

Place a sieve over a bowl and load it up with grapes. Using your fingers (gloved if you plan to drink the juice), squash the grapes through the mesh to make grape juice. Pour the juice into beakers and share it around.

Talk about the colour of the juice. What does it remind you of? Why do you think Jesus asked the disciples to remember him by sharing red wine?

3. POTATO PRINTING

You will need: standard-size potatoes, cut in half; cookie cutters (hearts, hands and feet); round-ended knives; spray-on or watered-down fabric paint in various colours on paper plates; white sheet big enough to use as a tablecloth

Encourage people to use the cookie cutters or knives to carve the flat side of the potatoes into various shapes associated with the Last Supper—hearts, hands, feet and goblets—and then, using the fabric paint, to stamp around the edges of the sheet to make a beautiful tablecloth. Try to encourage everyone from your Messy Church to add at least one stamp to the cloth.

Talk about the things you do that are unique to your family. Do you have any family traits or likenesses that set you apart? What is so special about being part of Jesus' family?

4. ACETATE FORGIVENESS

You will need: squares of acetate (10 cm x 10 cm); washable red felt pens; bowls of water; permanent black or green pens; wet wipes; towels

Invite people to write or draw things they are sorry for on the acetate in red felt pen. In bowls of water, wash the marks off—this will hopefully be a bit messy! Then, with permanent pen, write 'forgiven' or draw a smiley face on the acetate.

Talk about how it feels when we know we've done something wrong. How does it feel to be forgiven? Why do you think Jesus had to die in order for us to be forgiven for the wrong things we have done?

5. GLITTERING GOBLETS

You will need: empty 2-litre drink bottles; old CDs; gold or silver paint; PVA glue; glue gun; scissors

Cut around about a third of the way down from the top of the bottle using sharp scissors. With the glue gun, stick the bottle top onto a CD to make the base of the goblet. Mix some gold paint with glitter and a little PVA glue and paint your gorgeous glittery goblet.

Talk about Have you ever been out for a really posh meal? What was it like?

What kind of cup do you think Jesus and his friends would have shared?

Did they live big flashy lives or were they more humble and down to earth?

6. YUMMY SCRUMMY DINNER

You will need: paper plates; junk modelling bits; out-of-date dried pulses if available; lots of PVA glue; spreaders; paint; paintbrushes

Using paper plates, dried food, junk modelling bits and PVA glue, model your favourite meal, paint it and leave it to dry.

Talk about your favourite meal. What does your favourite meal remind you of? What would you cook if Jesus was coming to dinner?

SESSION MATERIAL: FEBRUARY

7. BREAD PUZZLES

You will need: tortilla wraps or pictures of various loaves of bread; paper plates

When the first person gets to your table, ask them to carefully tear a tortilla wrap or bread picture into ten or twelve shapes and put them on a plate. The next person who comes along needs to try to remake the puzzle before tearing another wrap or picture into a new puzzle for the next person.

Talk about how difficult it is to put the puzzle back together. Which is more fun, breaking the tortilla wrap or bread picture apart or puzzling out the puzzle? Why do you think Jesus broke the bread he gave to his disciples?

8. GRACE CUBES

You will need: cube nets cut out of cardboard; pens; colouring pencils

Invite households to work together to think of grace prayers to write on each side of the cube; each person should suggest at least one if possible. Make sure there is a prayer on each side of the cube and then decorate it appropriately. Have some traditional graces printed out for people to read in case they need a little inspiration. Households can then roll the cube at the beginning of each meal at home, and pray the prayer that lands on top. Why not try it out at your Messy meal together?

Talk about what sorts of things you chat about at dinner times. What do you think Jesus and his friends talked about at their last supper? What would it be like to pray together before each meal?

9. DOORFRAME

You will need: timber selection (with three bits big enough to make a doorframe); cardboard boxes; giant pieces of cardboard; carpet tubes; hammers; nails; saws; sticky tape; string, etc.

For this big build, to be used in the celebration, you need to construct a doorframe. Go to town with timber, saws, hammers and nails, if you're feeling brave, or simply make a frame big enough to walk through with cardboard boxes, carpet tubes and a big cardboard door. If you're going to use the door in

your celebration, you will need to add a hook to it for hanging signs on.

Talk about how inviting guests into our homes is fun. Who would you welcome in if you could welcome anyone? Is there anyone you'd feel nervous about letting into your house if they appeared at your door? Do you think the host was expecting Jesus and his friends to come for the Passover meal?

10. SOUR FACES

You will need: bunches of fresh parsley; bowls of salt water; sour sweets; lemon wedges

In deference to the Jewish custom at Passover, encourage people to dip a bunch of parsley into salt water to eat, or to try eating sour sweets and lemon wedges. Who can pull the best 'sour face' as they eat the different things available? If possible, you could take pictures of the sour faces to display during the celebration.

Talk about what makes you sad. Is there anything you're worrying about right now? Jesus seemed rather sad at the dinner table. Why do you think that was?

CELEBRATION

You will need: selection of signs with familiar symbols on and string attached for hanging; doorframe from activity 9

Place the doorframe at the front of the congregation and have the selection of signs to hand, ready to hang on the door hook. (If you didn't make a door, just hold up the signs as you speak.)

Who knows what a symbol is? It's a picture that tells us something we need to know or remember.

What would each of these signs mean if they were hanging on a door? *(In turn hang 'gents', 'ladies', 'no entry' and 'fire escape' signs on the door.)* There's a door in our story, but it didn't have any signs or symbols on it.

In fact, it was a very normal door in a city called Jerusalem, and behind the door lived a very normal man. He had a house with an upstairs room that he was very proud of.

  MessyChurchBRF   **MessyChurchBRF**   **@MessyChurchBRF**

Reprinted with permission from **Get Messy! Jan–Apr 2016**, published by Messy Church, a part of BRF

THE LAST SUPPER BY PETE MAIDMENT

On a very special day of the year called Passover, the man was just sitting down to lunch when there was a knock at the door. He got up, went to the door and opened it to find a group of friends standing in the street.

They looked at him. He looked at them. And then they said, 'The Rabbi says: "My appointed time is near. I am going to celebrate the Passover with my disciples at your house." '

The friends looked at the man. The man looked at the friends.

How did they know? he thought to himself. *How did they know about my room—because surely that's why they're here, to use my room to celebrate the Passover together. There are no signs or symbols on my door. How did they know?!*

The man was so surprised that he couldn't think of anything to say to the friends, except, 'You had better come in.'

And so the preparations began. They brought a beautiful tablecloth, cups and bowls. They brought bitter herbs and salt water for dipping. They brought bread made without yeast and wine.

The man recognised all these symbols. The tablecloth to represent a special meal. The bitter herbs to remind them of the Hebrews' sadness at being slaves in Egypt. The bread made without yeast to remind them of how the Hebrews had left Egypt in a hurry. The wine to represent freedom… and that it was going to be a fun evening!

The man was pleased to have his house used for such a special party and he hurried around making sure everyone was happy. He soon noticed that the friends seemed to be listening very carefully whenever one man in particular spoke—this must be the Rabbi they had referred to when they had knocked on his door earlier in the day.

As the man watched he saw, towards the end of the meal, the Rabbi doing a strange thing. He took the bread from the middle of the table, held it in the air, gave thanks for it and then broke it into pieces. 'This bread,' the Rabbi said, 'is a symbol of my body; take it and eat it.'

I wonder why he said, 'This bread is a symbol of my body,' thought the man.

Then the Rabbi took the wine from the table, gave thanks for it and said, 'This wine is a symbol of my blood; take it and drink it.'

I wonder why he said, 'This wine is a symbol of my blood,' thought the man.

But he was too busy to give it much thought, so he carried on bustling about until the party had finished. As everyone left he noticed how sad the Rabbi looked, which was a surprise after such a wonderful party. The man bade him farewell, shut the door and went back upstairs to start tidying up—wondering about everything he had seen.

PRAYER

Invite your Messy Church to be quiet for a moment, then read this reflection.

Remember a time when you felt happy.
Pause.
Thank you, Lord, for the good times.

Remember a time when you felt guilty.
Pause.
We're sorry, Lord, for the times we've let you down.

Remember a time when you felt sad.
Pause.
We praise you, Lord, that you promise to always be with us.

Amen

SONG SUGGESTIONS

'Our God is a great big God'—Jo Hemming and Nigel Hemming (Vineyard Songs)

'Bind us together'—Bob Gillman (Thankyou Music)

'My Jesus, my Saviour (Shout to the Lord)'—Darlene Zschech (Wondrous Worship)

MEAL SUGGESTION

A traditional lamb Passover meal may be a bit pricey, but shepherd's pie would fit just right, with a selection of fruit for afters!

MESSY REFLECTION

BECKY MAY

Very early on Sunday morning the women went to the tomb, carrying the spices they had prepared. They found the stone rolled away from the entrance to the tomb, so they went in; but they did not find the body of the Lord Jesus. They stood there puzzled about this, when suddenly two men in bright shining clothes stood by them. Full of fear, the women bowed down to the ground, as the men said to them, 'Why are you looking among the dead for one who is alive? He is not here; he has been raised. Remember what he said to you while he was in Galilee: "The Son of Man must be handed over to sinners, be crucified, and three days later rise to life."'

Then the women remembered his words, returned from the tomb, and told all these things to the eleven disciples and all the rest. The women were Mary Magdalene, Joanna, and Mary the mother of James; they and the other women with them told these things to the apostles. But the apostles thought that what the women said was nonsense, and they did not believe them. But Peter got up and ran to the tomb; he bent down and saw the grave cloths but nothing else. Then he went back home amazed at what had happened.

Luke 24:1–12 (GNT)

For those of us who have experienced church life for a number of years and enjoyed the cycle of seasons and repetition of stories, there becomes something familiar, or known, about the key narratives. As we approach the Easter season, we already know how the story ends; like a cosy jumper, we see it as a reassuring source of comfort, perhaps neglecting to stand in wonder at the great events as they unfold. It is almost as though we have gone straight to the last page of a new book rather than starting at the beginning, therefore missing something of the celebration when we reach Easter Sunday.

For the disciples, and others who were close to Jesus, what happened that first Easter was far from predictable. Even though Jesus had spoken to them about the events that would follow, it is entirely understandable that they were far from ready when the time came.

As the narrative unfolds, Easter morning brings one surprise after another: the privileged position of the women, rather than the men, in being the first to discover Jesus' disappearance; the movement of the stone; the startling appearance of angels; and the later discovery that Jesus had indeed been raised from the dead, and had ultimately beaten death itself.

As we approach this Easter season, spend some time praying that God would give you a fresh sense of awe and wonder for the events of this story; that you would enjoy the extraordinary narrative and celebrate the great surprises it holds, even today. As you prepare for this Messy Church, pray too for an opportunity to share this sense of awe and wonder with those you meet, as you explore the story together.

MEALTIME CARDS

- What is the strangest fact you have found out today?
- What is the most amazing thing you know about Jesus?
- Where do you think Jesus is now?

TAKE-HOME IDEA

At home, make and hide resurrection eggs for an Easter egg hunt with a twist.

You will need: twelve hollow plastic eggs that can be opened; marker pen; objects listed below; Bible verse printouts

Number the eggs, then place each of the following eleven items in an egg with the corresponding verse. The twelfth egg should remain empty apart from the verse.

1. Small green leaf
2. Piece of bread
3. Coin
4. Piece of string
5. Small thorn (use a twisted pipe cleaner if you prefer)
6. Cross (make one out of card or using toothpicks if you don't already have a small enough one)
7. Nails
8. Dice
9. Piece of sponge
10. Spear (Lego sword/toothpick, etc.)
11. Rock (small stone)

Hide the eggs in a trail around the house or in the garden. Look for them as a family and open each egg to look at the object inside. Ask the children if they know what it is or what it represents. Read each verse together and ask the children again what each object represents.

On Easter Sunday morning, enjoy some pastries as you read Luke 24:1–12 together as a family. Thank Jesus that he died and rose again to be your friend.

Reprinted with permission from **Get Messy! Jan–Apr 2016**, published by Messy Church, a part of BRF

UNBELIEVABLE TRUTH BY SIAN ASHFORD

1

2

3

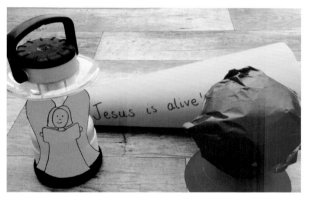

4

6

MESSY HEALTH CHECK

BRF's website **www.faithinhomes.org.uk** is a great resource for take-home ideas. What other sources of inspiration have you come across that will improve what you offer?

HOW DOES THIS SESSION HELP PEOPLE GROW IN CHRIST?

At Easter we celebrate the death and resurrection of Jesus. The Easter story reminds us that we are precious in God's sight—forgiven people who are offered hope in the most difficult situations—and that we are all part of a bigger picture and community. This session helps our Messy families to reflect on the resurrection and what it means for them in the light of other 'unbelievable truths', and encourages them to respond openly and honestly with their thoughts and questions.

BIBLE REFERENCE

Luke 24:1–12

MESSY TEAM THEME

- Imagine how the women may have felt at the tomb that morning. What words can you use to describe their feelings?
- Why do you think the apostles didn't believe the women? Do you think you would have believed them?
- What words describe how you feel when you come to Jesus?
- Is there anything about your faith, or any of God's promises, that you sometimes struggle to believe?

8

Reprinted with permission from **Get Messy! Jan–Apr 2016**, published by Messy Church, a part of BRF

SESSION MATERIAL: MARCH

ACTIVITIES

1. EASTER-MORNING SUNRISE

You will need: coffee filters; tray; food colouring (red, orange and yellow); tablespoon; water; small bowls; pipette or medicine syringe; sticky tape

Cut a coffee filter in half and place on the tray. Mix ten drops of one type of food colouring with one or two tablespoons of water in a small bowl. Repeat with the other two colours. Use the pipette or medicine syringe to drop one colour at a time on to the coffee filter. Continue until your filter is covered. Leave to dry and then hang in a window with some sticky tape.

Talk about your favourite time of day.

2. QUESTIONS, QUESTIONS

You will need: cardboard box with a letterbox-sized hole in the lid; pieces of paper; pens

Leave paper and pens on a table in a quiet part of the room where people can write down any questions they may have about the Easter story. Reassure them that it is fine to have questions and that no question is wrong. Invite them to post their questions into the box. Look at some of the questions during the celebration time.

Talk about how the disciples were Jesus' closest friends, yet they still didn't understand everything that happened to him and had questions to ask.

3. TOMB RACING

You will need: large open space; two starting markers; two footballs covered in black or brown paper; two large torches with a picture of an angel stuck on each; two card megaphones; stopwatch

Create an obstacle course by laying out the objects in the following order (you will need two sets so that people can race): starting markers, footballs (tombstones), torches (angels) and card megaphones. Leave space to run between each object. Contestants should race to the tombstone and roll it away, then run back to the marker; race to the angel and

shine the light, then run back to the marker; run to the megaphone and declare 'Jesus is alive!', then run back to the marker. You could time them on a stopwatch. The first one back wins.

Talk about how excited the women must have been to realise Jesus was alive.

4. PLANTING HERBS

You will need: pre-grown herbs; herb seeds (basil, parsley, chives, mint, etc.); peat-free compost; disposable pots or plastic cups; spoons to use as trowels; water in a little watering can or plastic bottle

Show the group the herbs that have already grown and encourage them to smell them. Tell them they are going to grow their own. Invite them to place some compost in one of the containers, then to add the herb seeds and cover them with more compost. Ask them to sprinkle some water on to the mixture, then give them care instructions.

Talk about how herbs are added to food to enhance flavour. When we add Jesus to our lives we are enhanced, too.

5. GRAFFITI WALL

You will need: lining paper; blu-tack; felt pens; laptop or phone; internet connection

Cover one wall with lining paper. Write in the middle of the paper: 'Jesus is back from the dead.' Invite the congregation to add their own amazing facts to the wall. It could be ones they already know or ones they search online to find.

Talk about which fact on the wall you find most amazing.

6. ROLLING STONES

You will need: chalk to draw a target on the floor with three or four concentric rings; selection of stones

Stand back from the target and roll the 'tombstones'. Can you roll them into the centre of the target?

Talk about what the tomb would have looked like. How big would the stone have been? What do you think was inside and outside the tomb? Was it a noisy or a quiet place?

UNBELIEVABLE TRUTH BY SIAN ASHFORD

7. EASTER SCAVENGERS

You will need: scavenger hunt sheet; small bag or container to collect items in; items to be found: something black, sticks, something red, cloth, rock, something empty, something white, something green and something new (ensure there are plenty of these to be found inside or outside the building)

DOWNLOAD

Scavenge around the building or outdoor area to find the items listed on the sheet. Bring your items back to show the leader when you are done.

Talk about what each item represents.

8. SPICY PAINTING

You will need: variety of ground spices (e.g. ginger, nutmeg, cinnamon, paprika); palette; water; paintbrushes; paper

Smell the different spices, then add each individually to a space in the palette. Add a small amount of water to each spice. Use the spice paints to paint a picture on the paper. Smell the picture once you have finished.

Talk about why you think the women took spices for Jesus' body.

9. NEW LIFE BUTTERFLY

You will need: small resealable food bags; pipe cleaners; different coloured tissue squares; googly eyes

Fill the sandwich bag with a selection of different coloured pieces of tissue paper. Ensure an even distribution across the bag. Fold a pipe cleaner in half and place the bag in between the two halves at the bend. Twist the pipe cleaners at the top of the bag to create wing shapes and antennae. Stick the eyes onto the pipe cleaners.

Talk about how caterpillars have new life as butterflies, and how Jesus' resurrection gives us access to new life too.

10. SHINY ANGEL BISCUITS

You will need: (makes 30 angels—adapt as necessary) two baking sheets; non-stick baking paper; mixing bowl; mixing spoon; 200 g butter; 100 g caster sugar; 300 g plain flour, plus extra for rolling; palette knife; rolling pin; clean surface for rolling; angel-shaped cutter; table knife; coloured boiled sweets; paper plates, pens and baking instruction sheets if not being cooked at Messy Church

(NB: check food packaging to ensure there are no traces of nuts)

If you have access to an oven, heat it to gas mark 3/160°C/140°C (fan). Line two baking sheets with non-stick baking paper. Cream the butter thoroughly and add the sugar. Beat together until fluffy. Add half the flour and mix thoroughly. Add the remaining flour and mix to a dough, binding it together with the palette knife. Knead the dough on a clean, floured surface until smooth. Carefully roll out the dough to the thickness of a one pound coin, then use the angel cutter to cut out your biscuits. With a table knife, cut a triangular shape out of the centre of each biscuit, then place them on the lined baking sheet, or individually on named paper plates if baking at home. Lightly crush the boiled sweets and place them in each triangular hole. If possible, bake for 20 minutes until golden. If this is not possible, give out instruction sheets for baking at home. Once baked, leave to cool and harden on the baking sheets.

Talk about what you think (or what the Bible says) angels really look like.

9

10

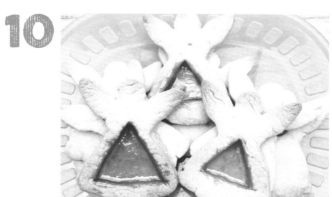

Reprinted with permission from **Get Messy! Jan–Apr 2016**, published by Messy Church, a part of BRF

SESSION MATERIAL: MARCH
UNBELIEVABLE TRUTH BY SIAN ASHFORD

CELEBRATION

You will need: cards with unbelievable truths written on; question box from activity 2; reflective music; copies of the 'empty tombs' template

DOWNLOAD

Before the celebration, ask the leaders to think of some unbelievable truths about themselves, for example, 'I once slept in an igloo.' Write a selection on small cards, including some untruths as well, and ask the leaders to read them out at the start of the celebration. Ask the congregation to stand up if they think what they are hearing is true.

Today we are going to hear a story about people who struggled to believe something they were told. See if you can join in with some actions.

It was very early in the morning. *(Yawn and stretch.)* Some women had been up all night preparing spices for Jesus' body. *(Make a bowl shape with one arm and stir with the other.)* As they approached the tomb they found the stone had been rolled away. They were shocked and confused. *(Look shocked and confused.)* They crept inside *(creep)*, but when they went in, they did not find Jesus' body. *(Search all around.)* They asked each other, 'What has happened?' *(Shrug and hold up your hands.)* While they were wondering about this, two men in shining clothes appeared beside them. *(Shield your eyes.)* The women were afraid and bowed their heads. *(Bow your head and look scared.)* The men said to them, 'Why are you looking for a living person in this place for the dead? He is not here; he has risen from the dead.' Then the women remembered what Jesus had said. *(Lightbulb moment.)* 'Oh yes, Jesus said he would be killed and would rise from the dead on the third day.' They began to get excited. 'Jesus is alive!' they exclaimed. *(Dance, jump around and cheer.)* They ran from the tomb *(run on the spot)* to find Jesus' followers to tell them the good news. *(Beckon them to come.)* The followers didn't believe them because it sounded like nonsense. *(Fold your arms and shake your head.)* But Peter got up and ran to the tomb. *(Run on the spot.)* Bending down and looking in, he saw the cloth that Jesus' body had been wrapped in. *(Bend down and make 'binoculars' with your hands to peer in.)* Peter went home, wondering what had happened.

So, you see, even Jesus' closest friend had questions about what had happened that morning. Jesus didn't mind that Peter wasn't sure and had to check for himself, and he doesn't mind if we have questions either.

Look in the question box from activity 2 and see what questions people have written. If you can, answer the questions; if you can't, be honest and say you don't know the answer. Explain that some questions are so big we may never know the answer, but it is still OK to ask them and talk to God about them in prayer.

PRAYER

Play some reflective background music. Hand out the empty tomb drawings. Ask people to write or draw something amazing about Jesus on an empty tomb. Close the celebration with this prayer.

Thank you, Jesus, for the amazing way you love us. Thank you that you love each one of us so much that you died and rose again so that we can be your friends. Please help us never to forget how amazing you are. Amen

SONG SUGGESTIONS

'Happy day'—Ben Cantelon and Tim Hughes (Thankyou Music)

'One, two, three'—Yancy (Dried Rose Music)

'Superhero'—Beci Wakerley and David Wakerley (Hillsong Music Publishing)

MEAL SUGGESTION

As we are celebrating the events of Easter morning, you could offer an all-day breakfast or bacon butties for the meal, followed by chocolate mousses (light and airy!)

f **MessyChurchBRF** **MessyChurchBRF** 🐦 **@MessyChurchBRF**

SESSION MATERIAL: APRIL
TWO TINY COINS BY BECKY MAY

MESSY REFLECTION

PETE MAIDMENT

Jesus looked around and saw rich people dropping their gifts in the Temple treasury, and he also saw a very poor widow dropping in two little copper coins. He said, 'I tell you that this poor widow put in more than all the others. For the others offered their gifts from what they had to spare of their riches; but she, poor as she is, gave all she had to live on.'
Luke 21:1–4 (GNT)

They're really annoying, aren't they? The flashy 'look at me' types who appear at the start of this story. You know the sort, in their over-the-top finery, gold this, diamond-encrusted that—no doubt riding the most up-to-date camel with all the extras. But it's OK: they give to charity; you can see them writing their cheques and starting their academies and foundations, generously donating a small percentage of their enormous wealth for the 'needy'. Not like you and me, normal people, who give what we can—well, a bit of what we can, providing it doesn't hurt too much and we still have enough left over for a decent cup of coffee on the way to work. Yet it's not the uber-generous or the fairly kind who catch Jesus' eye. Instead it's the mite-giver. It's the one who has almost nothing but gives anyway who Jesus notices and comments on.

Everyone likes to appear generous. We're used to grand displays of giving: the sponsored runs, the giant cheques on the TV charity night and the billionaire philanthropist working to eradicate disease in Africa. What doesn't get our attention is people with almost nothing giving more than they can afford for the benefit of others. By contrast, Jesus is unimpressed by the rich temple-goers with their huge donations. However, the poor widow with her tiny gift clearly touches his heart. Are we willing to risk being as generous as this one poor woman? What might Jesus be asking us to give?

Perhaps in our world the mite-giver is the widow in a war-torn country, who, as well as her own four or five children, cares for four or five more who have been orphaned. I wonder what Jesus says about her and her generosity. I wonder what we can learn from her.

MEALTIME CARDS

- If you could help any charity, what would it be and why?
- How can we give our gifts to God?
- Why do you think the widow gave the last of her money to God?

TAKE-HOME IDEA

Take your generosity jar from activity 9 home and put it in a place where everybody can see it. Talk about what you can do as a family to fill the jar, perhaps saving loose change, or everybody putting in a certain amount each week. As a family, decide who you would like to give the money to—perhaps a favourite charity. Talk to your Messy Church leaders for other ideas.

Dear God, thank you for all the things you give us. Help us to make kind choices about our money and possessions, so that we are not selfish, keeping all we own for ourselves, but remember to share with other people. Amen

SESSION MATERIAL: APRIL

3

5

7

8

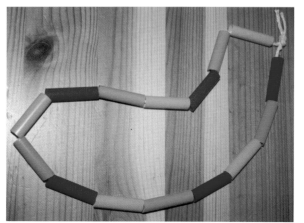

MESSY HEALTH CHECK

Would you say your planning meeting is purely practical, or is it also helpful to you spiritually? Could/should it be part of your walk with God?

HOW DOES THIS SESSION HELP PEOPLE GROW IN CHRIST?

This session offers a real challenge: that following God requires us to give all we have as our worship to him. This message runs contrary to the idea that we can give away a little, so long as we can still buy all the things we want for ourselves, and the story holds as much of a sting today as it did when Jesus and his disciples were standing in the Temple. The celebration is worded in such a way as to focus on the idea of giving to God, thus sensitively avoiding compounding the image that the church is there to take all your money.

BIBLE REFERENCE

Luke 21:1–4

MESSY TEAM THEME

- What can we do in our secret giving that God alone would notice?
- How can your involvement in Messy Church be offered as a sacrifice?
- What might Jesus notice if he stood with his disciples in the doorway to your Messy Church today?

9

TWO TINY COINS BY BECKY MAY

ACTIVITIES

1. DOWN THE CHUTE

You will need: cardboard tubes; cardboard boxes; wide sticky tape; scissors; sharp craft knife; pennies; nail varnish

Cut some cardboard tubes in half lengthways to create cardboard ramps, in an assortment of lengths. Stand a cardboard box up on one end, and use sticky tape to attach the tubes to the inside back wall of the box, at diagonal angles, so that one ramp leads to the next and so on, until they reach the bottom of the box. You could create an extra-large coin run with a larger box and sections of cardboard tube from the centre of wrapping paper, or rolls of fabric. Use pennies to test out the run, perhaps holding a race with two coins, one coloured with a spot of varnish to differentiate it!

Talk about the way that the lady in the story let go of her money and did not hold on tightly to it. She knew this was what God wanted her to do.

2. BIGGER, BIGGER!

You will need: plastic bottles; water; permanent marker pen; scissors; pictures for magnifying

Draw a circle at the top of the bottle, on the curved shoulder section, with the marker pen. Use the scissors to carefully cut this out to create a small curved dish. Pour a small amount of water into the dish. Place a selection of images on the table and look at how small they are. Put the 'magnifying dish' onto the pictures, to see how they appear larger when under the water.

Talk about how the onlookers saw the coins as a very small gift, but Jesus saw what it was really worth. To him it was much more valuable; much bigger.

3. CHOCOLATE COINS

You will need: giant chocolate buttons or chocolate discs; tubes of coloured writing icing

(NB: check food packaging to ensure there are no traces of nuts)

Design a coin by using the writing icing to add a value and draw a picture on to the chocolate buttons.

Talk about how different countries have different designs on their coins, often the head of the king or queen or something special to that country. Talk about the special designs people have used on their chocolate coins.

4. COIN TOWERS

You will need: large supply of loose change (1p and 2p coins work well); ruler

Stack the coins one on top of another to create the tallest tower you can, before it topples over. Measure how tall the tower is using the ruler, or count the coins as you go along.

Talk about how the rich people in the story would have had much, much more money left at home, but the widow in the story only had the little she gave away.

5. PURSES

DOWNLOAD

You will need: small pieces of coloured felt; templates A and B; pen; scissors; large sewing needles; embroidery thread; sticky backed hooks and loops

Draw around the two separate templates on to a piece of felt, then cut out the shapes. Using a needle and thread, sew the front and back sections together by stitching around the lower curved edge of the purse, using small overlapping stitches to secure each end of the thread. Stick a hook on to the front of the purse and a loop on to the top flap so that it can be folded over to fasten the purse shut.

Talk about why we use a purse or wallet to keep our money safe when we are away from home. Perhaps the widow in the story kept her coins in a purse.

6. OPTICAL ILLUSIONS

You will need: selection of optical illusion images, including those involving a size comparison and those where things are not what they seem at first glance (these can be sourced online)

Display optical illusions around the room for people to try to solve.

SESSION MATERIAL: APRIL

Talk about what happens when you first look at the pictures, and the way one thing can appear to be true, but when you look closer, you can see something else is actually true. When the disciples first saw the woman putting her money into the pot, it looked like she was giving very little, but when they looked more closely, Jesus showed them she was giving everything she had.

7. WOODEN-SPOON PUPPETS

You will need: wooden spoons; selection of fabrics, wool, sequins, etc.; children's Bible illustrations showing typical clothing from Jesus' time; scissors; PVA glue; spreaders; felt pens

Use the fabrics provided to create clothes for a wooden-spoon puppet, deciding whether the character is poor, like the widow in the story, or rich, and dressing them appropriately. Add hair and draw facial features on to the spoon.

Talk about how Jesus and the disciples could tell if people were rich just by looking at them. Perhaps they were wearing very fancy clothes to show off their wealth.

8. BEADED JEWELLERY

You will need: elasticated cord; scissors; sticky tape; drinking straws cut into short sections; dried pasta tubes dyed with food colouring; assorted beads

Cut the cord to an appropriate length for making a necklace or a bracelet, and stick one end to the table with tape. Select beads, pieces of straw and pasta tubes to thread on to the cord. Carefully unstick the cord and tie the two ends of the cord together to secure.

Talk about how the rich people showed off their wealth, perhaps by wearing fancy clothes or expensive jewellery.

9. GENEROSITY JAR

You will need: cleaned plastic tubs (such as those used for laundry capsules, drinking chocolate or milkshake powder); craft knife; stickers; sequins; coloured card; PVA glue; spreaders; scissors

Use the craft knife to carefully cut a slot in the top of a tub, large enough for coins to fall through. Decorate the tub using the stickers, sequins and cut-outs from the coloured card. The jar can then be used at home to save money together as a family, to give to a charity or a good cause.

Talk about why we should share what we have been given with others, making life better for people who do not have as much as we do. Talk about any charities that are particularly well known within your Messy Church and how you can support them.

10. PRAYER CONTAINER

You will need: circles of yellow card; pens; large container such as a bucket or cardboard box

On the yellow card 'coins' write or draw something you can do for God as your gift to him. Place them in the large container.

Talk about how we can show God our gratitude or appreciation in many ways, not just by giving our money. It might be giving our time to help at Messy Church, or using our gifts or skills, such as playing a musical instrument in the celebration time.

TWO TINY COINS BY BECKY MAY

CELEBRATION

You will need: rich and poor wooden-spoon puppets from activity 7 (you may need to prepare a poor one in advance in case people choose not to make this kind); prayer container from activity 10

Today, we are thinking about something that happened when Jesus was on earth. This isn't a story about a miracle, or even a parable. This is the story of something that caught Jesus' attention, something he noticed when he was out with his disciples. When they saw what happened, they learned a very important lesson, just as we can today.

One day, Jesus and his disciples were in the Temple, which was the special place where God's followers went to worship God and learn more about him. It was a bit like us coming here to Messy Church. In the Temple, there was a special box, perhaps a bit like this one *(hold up the prayer container)*, where everybody could put their gifts of money. Whenever people put money in the box, it was like they were giving a gift to God. The money could perhaps be used to help poor people, or to buy something that was needed in the Temple in order to carry on telling people about God.

While they were standing near the box, Jesus told his disciples to look closely at what was happening. First, some very rich people came by. *(Invite those who have made a wealthy-looking wooden-spoon puppet to hold it up at this point.)* Look at them all with their beautiful, expensive clothes and sparkly jewellery. Look at all the beautiful colours and patterns on their clothes. Actually, these very rich people liked it when everybody noticed them, so they stood up tall and proud and put their money into the box. Perhaps it was a few gold coins; it was certainly a lot of money. But even though they gave a lot of money, they still had lots and lots more money left!

Then came along a little old lady. *(Invite anyone who made a poorer-looking puppet to hold this up.)* She didn't have fancy clothes or expensive jewellery, and she didn't want other people to notice her. She didn't have lots of gold coins to give—just two tiny coins. This lady wanted to put her money into the box quietly, so that only God would see.

However, Jesus noticed the lady's tiny coins going into the box. Then he said to his disciples, 'I wonder who you think gave the most money today. It looked like the rich people gave the most money, didn't it? Their money was certainly worth more than the lady's two tiny coins.' But Jesus went on to tell his disciples that the old lady's gift was far more precious than all those gold coins put together! I wonder if you know why. You see, the rich people had so much money they wouldn't miss the coins they put into the box. They could still buy anything they wanted with the money they had left over. But the little old lady had nothing left. She had given her only coins to the Temple as her gift to God.

We can give things to God, too. Perhaps we have some money we could give to a charity that helps people and shows them God's love. Perhaps we could collect our empty boxes and other useful junk to use here at Messy Church. Perhaps we could give some of our toys or clothes to a charity shop. And when we do give something away, perhaps we should remember today's story and try to be like the old lady, who quietly gave God everything she had, rather than showing off, like the rich people in their expensive clothes.

PRAYER

Bring out the prayer container from activity 10.

Lord Jesus, you give us so many wonderful things: families to love us; friends to play with; homes where we feel safe; food to help us grow strong; and stories we can learn from. Thank you for all these gifts. Today, we give back to you our gifts of singing and dancing, cooking and cleaning, teaching and creating; may these be as precious to you as those two tiny coins in today's story. Amen

SONG SUGGESTIONS

'Giving everything'—Pete James (Hillsong Music Publishing)

'You can reach out with a heart of love'—Doug Horley (Thankyou Music)

MEAL SUGGESTION

Sausages, jacket potatoes and sweetcorn (gold coins), followed by fruit salad

Advice for Messy Church leaders from Jane Leadbetter

Dear Jane

Tony from Greater London writes:

Hi. I'm a leader in our Messy Church and I'm also our Boys' Brigade Captain. As part of the BB we have regular church parades. Sadly attendances at the church parades are really falling; however, conversely, Messy Church is stable in numbers and possibly increasing. So my questions are, do you think a Messy Church parade would work? Has it been tried elsewhere, and do you think there are any barriers to doing this? As BB Captain it is my role to introduce children to God and I think this could be good way.

Hi Tony

Ooh, one of my favourite subjects—church parades! In addition to being a Messy Church coordinator I am also a Scout leader of some 20 years and counting, and I attend monthly church parades with my Beaver Scouts. We piloted a Messy Sunday in July a few years ago that combined our Messy Church and church parade congregations. It was great! It is now expected every year and the church puts on a barbecue afterwards. Other church parades have also become like Messy Church with the integration of activities. We have approximately seven safe spaces we can use in church, and each uniformed section helps to run the activities. We involve the Guides, too. In a typical Messy Church parade service of an hour we have 20 minutes for activities on the theme. We process our flags and give out badges. The children's parents and carers come too! Our termly programme includes visiting Messy Church each month, which links to lots of badges! Email me for any more information jane.leadbetter@brf.org.uk

Hi Sheila

How exciting for you! Lots of prayers as you prepare for your Messy journey in your community.

Things to consider for your Messy Church team. Do you need to look 'team'? What does this convey to your community? Is the team 'delivering' church or 'being' church together, all ages, all at different stages, but all on the same journey? If you decide to look 'team', do you have young people on the team who are also willing to wear the T-shirts?

Sheila from Coventry writes:

We start our first Messy Church soon. Should we invest some money in purchasing Messy Church 'uniform' for the Messy Church team? There are twelve of us and we were thinking of T-shirts. Where is the best place to find them?

As members of the BRF Messy Church team we have visited many Messy Churches and discovered teams in bright T-shirts with the Messy Church logo on the front, colour-schemed to match the bright new banner and napkins! We have seen teams with big, bold Messy badges, and also teams with Messy Church hats! We have also visited Messy Churches where the teams have naturally blended in and are engaged with the activities and Messy congregation. Maybe they have worn their names on labels the same as the Messy congregation.

If you choose to purchase clothing items such as T-shirts, hoodies and aprons, then CPO (Christian Publishing and Outreach) stock the Messy Church range, including Messy Church mugs and key rings. The hoodies are especially popular! www.cpo.org.uk/messychurch

It was lovely to receive the following from Val in Surrey:

Hi Jane. Just to let you know that we followed your useful advice: set up a social media page; sent out invitations to the children's groups that meet in our hall; sent texts, emails and paper invitations to all those families who had come before; tweaked our posters to say exactly what we were doing; and asked the congregation to pray. And... 35 families turned up! So thank you so much for your encouragement and support. The team is very encouraged and keen to continue. We are going to change our welcome slightly next time, too. We also had a visit from the neighbouring All Saints Church!

Email jane.leadbetter@brf.org.uk with your Messy questions. Do get in touch for any advice.

 f MessyChurchBRF   **(P)** MessyChurchBRF   **🐦** @MessyChurchBRF